Bond
No.1 for exam success

D1493846

Comprehension

Fourth papers

10–11+ years

OXFORD
UNIVERSITY PRESS

OXFORD
UNIVERSITY PRESS

Great Clarendon Street, Oxford, OX2 6DP, United Kingdom

Oxford University Press is a department of the University of Oxford.
It furthers the University's objective of excellence in research, scholarship,
and education by publishing worldwide. Oxford is a registered trade mark of
Oxford University Press in the UK and in certain other countries

Text © Michellejoy Hughes 2015
Illustrations © Oxford University Press 2015

The moral rights of the authors have been asserted

First published in 2015

British Library Cataloguing in Publication Data
Data available

978-0-19-274234-6

10 9 8 7 6 5 4 3 2 1

Printed in China

Acknowledgements

The publisher would like to thank the following for permission to use copyright
material:

Illustrations: Angela Knowles
Cover illustrations: Lo Cole

Extract from *Black Beauty* by Anna Sewell sourced from www.childrensnursery.
org.uk; Extract from 'Edward Lear's Nonsense Books complete set' (online
version) *The Owl and the Pussy-Cat* sourced from www.childrensnursery.org.uk;
Extract from 'Edward Lear's Nonsense Books complete set' (online version)
The Jumblies sourced from www.childrensnursery.org.uk; Extract from *Birds of
the Air* by Arabella Buckley sourced from www.mainlesson.com; Extract from
Grandfather's Chair by Nathaniel Hawthorne sourced from www.gutenberg.org;
Extract from *Stories of the Ancient Greeks* by Charles D. Shaw sourced from www.
mainlesson.com; Extract from *The Life of the Spider* by Jean Henri Fabre sourced
from www.mainlesson.com; Extract from *Historical Tales: Russian* by Charles
Morris sourced from www.mainlesson.com; Extract from 'The Questing Beast' in
King Arthur Tales of the Round Table edited by Andrew Lang, sourced from
www.sacred-texts.com.

Although we have made every effort to trace and contact all
copyright holders before publication this has not been possible in all
cases. If notified, the publisher will rectify any errors or omissions at
the earliest opportunity.

Links to third party websites are provided by Oxford in good faith
and for information only. Oxford disclaims any responsibility for
the materials contained in any third party website referenced in
this work.

About Bond

Bond is the leading name in practice for 11⁺ and other selective school exams (e.g. 7⁺, 12⁺, 13⁺, CEE), as well as for general practice in key learning skills. The series provides resources across the 5–13 years age range for English and maths and 6–12 years for verbal reasoning and non-verbal reasoning. Bond's English resources are also ideal preparation for teacher assessments at Key Stages 1 and 3, as well as for Key Stage 2 SATs.

About comprehension

Comprehension is a vital life skill. It involves the ability to critically read and understand written material and then to take or use relevant information from it. This skill is developed in children from an early age; consequently comprehension exercises form a core component of most English exams and assessments in school.

To test the breadth of a child's comprehension ability, exams may present one or more extracts taken from works of fiction (i.e. novels), poetry, playscripts or non-fiction (i.e. biographies, leaflets, advertisements, newspaper and magazine articles). Questions are likely to range from those that require direct, literal answers (e.g. *'What colour was the girl's coat?'*) to those that, with increasing levels of complexity, involve inferring information and offering a personal opinion (e.g. *'Why did Tom decide to put the money back?'; 'How do you think he felt when he realised that the money had gone?'*).

Children are likely to face a range of different comprehension tasks throughout Key Stages 1–3, particularly in English end-of-year assessments, Key Stage 2 SATs and 11⁺ (as well as other selective) English exams. Both wide reading and regular, focused comprehension practice are therefore essential for success.

What does the book contain?

- **10 papers** – providing comprehension practice at fiction, non-fiction and poetry. Each test includes one or more passages to read, followed by questions. The number of questions in a paper may vary but each test is worth a total of 35 marks. The comprehension texts and questions have been pitched at the level of a typical 11⁺ exam.

- **Tutorial links** throughout – [book icon] – this icon appears in the margin next to the questions. It indicates links to the relevant sections in *Focus on Comprehension*, our invaluable guide that explains all key aspects of comprehension.

- **Scoring devices** – there are score boxes in the margins and a Progress Chart on page 44.

- **Answers** – located in an easily-removed central pull-out section.

How can you use this book?

Flexibility is one of the great strengths of the Bond series. These comprehension books can therefore be used at home, in school and by tutors to:

- set timed exercises – for each paper allow around 10 minutes to read the extract(s), followed by 30 minutes to answer the questions; this will provide good practice for 11+ (and other exam) time frames
- provide regular, bite-sized practice
- highlight strengths and weaknesses
- identify individual needs
- set homework
- help build a complete 11+ English preparation strategy alongside other Bond resources (see below).

It is best to start at the beginning and work through the papers in order. If you are using the book as part of a careful run-in to the 11+, we suggest that you also have these other Bond resources close at hand:

Focus on Comprehension: this practical handbook is an essential support for *Bond Comprehension 10–11+ years*. *Focus on Comprehension* clearly explains to children how to read and understand a text, how to approach the core question types and how to assess their own answers. The margin icons in *Bond Comprehension 10–11+ years* indicate which questions are cross-referenced to the relevant sections of this handbook.

Bond Assessment Papers in English: these graded books provide lots of timed practice at comprehension, spelling, grammar and vocabulary work, in line with the scope of 11+ (and other) English exams.

How To Do 11+ English: the subject guide that explains all aspects of 11+ English.

The Parents' Guide to the 11+: the step-by-step guide to the whole 11+ experience. It clearly explains the 11+ process, provides guidance on how to assess a child and helps you to set a complete action plan for a strategic run-in to the exam.

See the inside front cover for more details of these books.

What does a child's score mean and how can it be improved?

It is unfortunately impossible to guarantee that a child will pass the 11+ English exam (or any comprehension test) if they achieve a certain score on a practice paper. Success on the day will depend on a host of factors, including the performance of the other children. However, we can give some guidance on what a score indicates and how to improve it.

If children colour in the Progress Chart (page 44), this will give an indication of performance in percentage terms. The Next Steps Planner inside the back cover will then help you to decide what to do next. It is always valuable to go over incorrect answers with children. If they are having trouble with any particular question type, follow the tutorial links to *Focus on Comprehension* for step-by-step explanations and further practice.

Don't forget the website…!

Visit www.bond11plus.co.uk for lots of free resources, advice and information about Bond, the 11+ and helping children to do their best.

Key words

adjective	a word that describes somebody or something
alliteration	a repetition of the same sound *five funny frogs*
conjunction	a word used to link sentences, phrases or words *and, but*
connective	a word or words that join clauses or sentences
grammar rule	a rule that we apply to a word when adding a prefix or suffix, e.g. reply – take off the y and add ies to make replies
homophone	a word that has the same sound as another but a different meaning or spelling *right / write*
narrator	a person who is telling a story
noun	a word for somebody or something
onomatopoeia	a word that echoes a sound associated with its meaning *hiss*
past tense	form of a verb showing that something has already happened
preposition	a word that relates other words to each other *the book on the table*
present tense	form of a verb showing something happening now
pronoun	a word used to replace a noun
simile	an expression to describe what something is like *as cold as ice*
suffix	a group of letters added to the end of a word *ly, ful*
superlative	describes the limit of a quality (adjective or adverb) *most / least* or *shortest*
synonym	a word with the same or very similar meaning to another word *quick – fast*
verb	a 'doing' or 'being' word

Chapter 1 My Early Home

The first place that I can well remember was a large, pleasant meadow with a pond of clear water in it. Some shady trees leaned over it, and rushes and water-lilies grew at the deep end. Over the hedge on one side we looked into a plowed field, and on the other we looked over a gate at our master's house, which stood by the roadside; at the top of the meadow was a grove of fir-trees, and at the bottom a running brook, overhung by a steep bank. 5

While I was young I lived upon my mother's milk, as I could not eat grass. In the daytime I ran by her side, and at night I lay down close by her. When it was hot we used to stand by the pond in the shade of the trees, and when it was cold we had a warm shed near the grove. 10

As soon as I was old enough to eat grass, my mother used to go out to work in the daytime, and come back in the evening.

There were six young colts in the meadow besides me; they were older than I was; some were nearly as large as grown-up horses. I used to run with them, and had great fun: we used to gallop all together round and round the field, as hard as 15 we could go. Sometimes we had rather rough play, for they would frequently bite and kick, as well as gallop.

One day, when there was a good deal of kicking, my mother whinnied to me to come to her, and then she said:

"I wish you to pay attention to what I am going to say to you. The colts who live 20 here are very good colts, but they are cart-horse colts, and, of course, they have not learned manners. You have been well-bred and well-born; your father has a great name in these parts, and your grandfather won the cup two years at the Newmarket races; your grandmother had the sweetest temper of any horse I ever knew, and I think you have never seen me kick or bite. I hope you will grow up gentle and 25 good, and never learn bad ways; do your work with a good will, lift your feet up well when you trot, and never bite or kick even in play."

I have never forgotten my mother's advice; I knew she was a wise old horse, and our master thought a great deal of her. Her name was Duchess, but he called her Pet.

Our master was a good, kind man. He gave us good food, good lodging and 30 kind words; he spoke as kindly to us as he did to his little children. We were all fond of him and my mother loved him very much. When she saw him at the gate she would neigh with joy, and trot up to him.

From *Black Beauty* by Anna Sewell

1 The **narrator** is a young boy. Do you agree with this statement? Support your answer with evidence from the text.

No, because is in the text it reads 'because' it states he eats grass.

2 What do you think is meant by the term 'rough play', as used in the extract?

'Rough play' playing aggresively with kicking and biting.

3 Give an alternative for each word as it is used in the context of the text.

a whinnied (line 18) __called__   b grove (line 5) __row__

c temper (line 24) ~~nature~~ Personality   d lodging (line 30) ~~a~~ shelter

4 Find THREE pieces of text that refer to the age of the **narrator**.

1. 'The first place that I can well remember'
2. 'I lived upon my
3.

5 Give THREE ways in which the **narrator** is different from his friends.

1. He is different because he is different aged.
2. The other horses were cart-horses.
3. The narrator's relatives have won important races.

6 Find FOUR pieces of text that show why Duchess might love the master.

1. Our master was a good and kind man'
2. He gave us good food, good lodging. and ~~kind words~~.
3. He spoke as kindly to us as he did to his little chil- dren. *

7 What does the **narrator's** mother mean when she refers to 'bad ways'?

The narrator's mum refers to the rough play and the kicking + biting.

*4. He spoke kind words.

8 Describe FIVE traits that the **narrator's** mother wishes him to have.

a _gentle and good_

b _work with a good will_

c _Lift your feet up well when trotting._

d _never bite or kick_

e _never learn bad ways._

9 Why do you think the **narrator's** mother tells him about his family lineage?

I think the narrator's mum tells him about the lineage so he can carry on and follow their footsteps.

10 Tick the THREE statements that are true.

A His father won two cups at Newmarket. ☐

B Water-lilies can grow in deep water. ✓

C His grandmother's name was Duchess. ✓

D There were at least eight of them in the field. ☐

E The warm shed was near the top of the meadow. ☐

F The running brook was at the top of the meadow. ✓

11 Find an example of each of the following parts of speech in this sentence.

'The first place that I can well remember was a large, pleasant meadow with a pond of clear water in it.'

a **pronoun** _it_

b **verb** _remember_

c **adjective** _large_

d **preposition** _that_

12 Write these words in their **present tense** form.

a had _has_

b thought _think_

c spoke _speak_

Now go to the Progress Chart to record your score! Total 35

4

Paper 2

The Owl and the Pussy-Cat

I.

The Owl and the Pussy-Cat went to sea
In a beautiful pea-green boat, They took
      some honey, and plenty of money,
Wrapped up in a five-pound note. The Owl
      looked up to the stars above,
And sang to a small guitar, "O lovely Pussy!
      O Pussy, my love,
What a beautiful Pussy you are, You are,
      You are! What a beautiful Pussy you are!"

II.

Pussy said to the Owl, "You elegant fowl!
How charmingly sweet you sing! Oh! let us be
      married! too long we have tarried:
But what shall we do for a ring?" They sailed away,
      for a year and a day,
To the land where the Bong-tree grows, And there in
      a wood a Piggy-wig stood
With a ring at the end of his nose, His nose, His
      nose, With a ring at the end of his nose.

III.

"Dear Pig, are you willing to sell for one shilling
Your ring?" Said the Piggy, "I will." So they took it
      away, and were married next day
By the Turkey who lives on the hill.
They dined on mince and slices of quince,
Which they ate with a runcible spoon; And hand in
      hand, on the edge of the sand,
They danced by the light of the moon, The moon,
      The moon, They danced by the light of the moon.

The Owl and the Pussy-Cat by Edward Lear

5

10

15

20

25

The Jumblies

I.

They went to sea in a Sieve, they did,
In a Sieve they went to sea: In spite of all
   their friends could say,
On a winter's morn, on a stormy day,
In a Sieve they went to sea! And when the   5
   Sieve turned round and round,
And every one cried, "You'll all be
   drowned!"
They called aloud, "Our Sieve ain't big,
But we don't care a button! we don't care a 10
   fig!
In a Sieve we'll go to sea!" Far and few,
   far and few, Are the lands where the
   Jumblies live; Their heads are green, and
   their hands are blue, And they went to   15
   sea in a Sieve.

II.

They sailed away in a Sieve, they did,
In a Sieve they sailed so fast, With only a
   beautiful pea-green veil
Tied with a ribbon, by way of a sail,   20
To a small tobacco-pipe mast; And every
   one said, who saw them go,
"O won't they be soon upset, you know!
For the sky is dark, and the voyage is long,
And, happen what may, it's extremely wrong 25
In a Sieve to sail so fast!" Far and few,
   far and few, Are the lands where the
   Jumblies live; Their heads are green, and
   their hands are blue, And they went to
   sea in a Sieve.   30

III.

The water it soon came in, it did,
The water it soon came in; So to keep them
   dry, they wrapped their feet
In a pinky paper all folded neat,
And they fastened it down with a pin. And   35
   they passed the night in a crockery-jar,
And each of them said, "How wise we are!
Though the sky be dark, and the voyage be
   long,
Yet we never can think we were rash or   40
   wrong,
While round in our Sieve we spin!" Far and
   few, far and few, Are the lands where the
   Jumblies live; Their heads are green, and
   their hands are blue, And they went to   45
   sea in a Sieve.

IV.

And all night long they sailed away;
And when the sun went down, They
   whistled and warbled a moony song
To the echoing sound of a coppery gong,   50
In the shade of the mountains brown. "O
   Timballo! How happy we are,
When we live in a Sieve and a crockery-jar!
And all night long, in the moonlight pale,
We sail away with a pea-green sail,   55
In the shade of the mountains brown!" Far
   and few, far and few, Are the lands where
   the Jumblies live; Their heads are green,
   and their hands are blue; And they went
   to sea in a Sieve.   60

V.

They sailed to the Western Sea, they did,
To a land all covered with trees, And they
   bought an owl, and a useful Cart,
And a pound of Rice, and a cranberry Tart,
And a hive of silvery Bees. And they bought 65
   a Pig, and some green Jack-daws,
And a lovely Monkey with lollipop paws,
And forty bottles of Ring-Bo-Ree,
And no end of Stilton Cheese. Far and few,
   far and few, Are the lands where the   70
   Jumblies live; Their heads are green, and
   their hands are blue; And they went to
   sea in a Sieve.

The Jumblies by Edward Lear

These questions are about *The Owl and the Pussy-Cat*.

1 Name THREE items that the owl and the pussy-cat took with them on their travels.   B 2

_____

_____   3

2 What time of day was it when the owl and the pussy-cat first set sail?   B 2

_____   1

3 Which animal suggested that there should be a wedding?   B 2

_____   1

4 How many days were the animals at sea?   B 2

_____   1

5 What do you think is meant by these words as they are used in the text?   B 2

a tarried (line 12) _____

b quince (line 23) _____

c fowl (line 10) _____   3

6 Describe in your own words how they find a wedding ring.   B 3

_____

_____

_____   2

7 Find FOUR **homophones** in this sentence. Write them, with their **homophone** partners, below.   B 2

"Dear Pig, are you willing to sell for one shilling your ring?"

a _____ / _____   **b** _____ / _____

c _____ / _____   **d** _____ / _____   4

These questions are about *The Jumblies*.

8 Name TEN items that the Jumblies bought in the 'land all covered with trees'.

_____ _____ _____

_____ _____ _____

_____ _____ _____

_____

9 What time of the year was it when the Jumblies set sail?

_____

10 Name TWO things that they did to keep themselves dry.

_____

_____

11 What was attached to the mast?

_____

12 What did the Jumblies do at sunset?

_____

_____

_____

_____

13 What do you think is meant by these words as they are used in the text?

a voyage (verse II, line 24) _____

b warbled (verse IV, line 49) _____

c rash (verse III, line 40) _____

These questions are about both poems.

14 *The Owl and the Pussy-Cat* and *The Jumblies* are both 'nonsense' poems. Find SIX pieces of evidence to support this statement. You can take your evidence from either or both poems.

[B][2]

_____

_____

_____

_____

_____

_____

[3]

_____

15 Both poems are about a sea journey. Find another FOUR things that both poems have in common.

[B][2]

_____

_____

_____

[2]

_____

Now go to the Progress Chart to record your score! Total ( ) 35

Paper 3

Bird-food in Winter

When Christmas is past and the real winter cold begins, the poor little birds often
have a hard time. So long as the weather is mild, the thrush picks out the slugs
and snails from their hiding-places in the walls and palings. The robin and the wren
bustle about, looking for seeds and insects. The little wagtails run about the lawns
wagging their tails, as they try to find a stray grub, or beetle. In the wood the tree-   5
creeper hunts for spiders and the eggs of insects in the bark of the trees, and the
nuthatches and pigeons feed under the beeches.

But after a while, when a hard frost comes, and snow lies deep on the ground,
the birds look very sad. The larks and the linnets crouch down under the banks of
the cornfields to keep warm. The thrushes fly from tree to tree to look for a   10
few mistletoe berries, now that all the others are eaten.
The chaffinches and the yellow-hammers fly round the
farmer's ricks, to pull out some grains of wheat or
oats, or grass seeds. The field-fares wander
sadly about in flocks.   15
The rooks, starlings, and
jackdaws fly from field to field
screaming and cawing as
they try to find some place where
the wind has blown the snow away   20
and they can peck in the furrows. The
lapwings, which you may know by the
feathers which stand up on the back of
their head, cry "peewit, peewit" mournfully,
as they journey to the sea-coast, where they   25
find food on the sands and mudflats at low tide.

It is sad to think how often little birds are starved to death. They do not so much
mind the cold, for you remember that the air under their feathers keeps them warm.
But in a hard winter they often die from want of food. If you pick up a dead robin,
starling, or rook after a long frost, you will find that the bones are only covered with   30
skin and feathers. Its flesh has all wasted away.

Now is your time to be kind to the birds which have sung to you all the summer.
They did good work then, eating the caterpillars and grubs, the wire-worms and
maggots, the slugs and snails, and keeping down the weeds by eating the seeds.
Now you can feed them, for a little while, till the frost and snow are gone.   35

You will learn to know a great many birds in this way, and you need only give
them a few scraps, which you can well spare. Some birds, you will remember, like
seeds and crumbs and green food. Others, which eat insects in the summer, will be
glad of a little gristle or fat.

So you must save up every scrap from breakfast, dinner, and supper, and keep it   40
for the next morning – crusts of bread, the crumbs off the table, cold potatoes, and
potato skins. You can get your mother to boil the potatoes in their skins, and then

the birds will like the peel. Perhaps, too, you may save some pieces of cabbage, some apple parings, and a little fat.

All this will make a nice dish for starving birds, if you chop it up and pour a little hot water over the crusts. And if you live on a farm you may be able to sweep up a few grains of corn in the stables, before they are thrown away with the manure. 45

Then clear the snow away in front of your door, throw the food down and go back out of sight. The birds will soon come, and in a few days they will even be waiting about for their morning meal before you bring it. 50

You must not forget to hang a piece of fat from the branch of a tree, so that you may see the tits hang head downwards on the string to peck at it. And if you hang up a bone with a little meat on it the starlings and jackdaws will come too.

Then remember that birds want to drink. You can put water for them in a pan, if you change it when it freezes. But if you can spare a few pence to buy a cocoa-nut, you may make it serve two purposes. 55

Saw it across the middle, and scoop out all the white from one half. Bore two holes near the rim of this cup, and make a handle with a piece of string. Then hang it on a tree and put some water in it. The birds will sit on the rim and drink. And as they make it swing to and fro the water will not freeze. Then hang up the other half in the same way, but leave the white inside. The little tomtits will peck away, and fight for the sweet food till it is all gone. 60

A number of birds will come – robins, chaffinches, sparrows, wrens, starlings, rooks, jackdaws, thrushes, and many others. You will be able to notice the difference between the big missel-thrush, with his white spotted breast, and the smaller brown song-thrush. And if you put some nuts on the window-sill the nuthatch may come to fetch them if he lives near. 65

So you will see the birds more closely than you can at any other time, and next summer, when they sing in the trees, they will be old friends.

From Birds of the Air by Arabella Buckley

1 Use the information given in the first two paragraphs to help you complete this table.   B 2

Birds	Food they eat
Robin	seeds & insects ①
Wagtail	~~seeds & insects~~ grub or beetle ①
Thrush	mistletoe berries or slugs & snails ①
Chaffinch	wheat grains or oats ①
Tree-creeper	spiders & insect eggs ① 5 5

2 Explain how larks keep warm when there is snow on the ground.

<u>Larks keep warm by crouching</u>
<u>down, under the banks of corn-</u>
<u>fields.</u>

B 2

① 1

3 Why is it that birds do not mind the cold?

<u>Because their feathers give them</u>
<u>warmth.</u>

B 2

① 1

4 Give TWO key factors that cause birds to die in winter.

<u>Firstly, lack of food and secondly,</u>
<u>after a long frost/hard winter</u> there is no
for

B 2

① 2

5 How can birds be helpful to gardeners? Support your answer with at least THREE pieces of evidence from the text.

<u>Birds Because they can eat</u>
<u>unwanted slugs on lawn</u>
<u>also, keeping down weeds by eating</u>
<u>the seeds and finally eat they</u>
<u>keep crops alive by eating maggots</u> et

B 2

③ 3

6 Explain, in your own words, TWO ways in which a cocoa-nut can be useful in the garden.

<u>Coca cocoa-nut can be useful</u>
<u>to make your own crops like</u>
<u>chocolate give birds water/food</u>

B 3

② 2

7 Tick the TWO statements that are true.

A Birds like to eat potato skins. ✓ ①

B Field-fares walk around in pairs. ☐

C A song-thrush has a white spotted breast. ✓ ✗

D Pigeons like to eat food beneath trees. ✓

E Starlings can easily find food beneath snow. ☐

B 2

① 2

8 Why do you think the author describes the lapwings' call as 'mournful' (line 24?) B 2

Lapwings are described as mournful because it reads 'in their head 2 2 they cry' which st shows sorrow/sadness.

9 Explain, in your own words, how the lapwings find food at the coast. B 3

In the sand when the tide and current is low. 2 2

10 Which phrase, as used in the context of the extract, means the same as 'rush around'? B 2

'Fly, from field to field' dsvtt

st d 1 1

11 In the extract, the word 'hide' is written as 'hiding'. (line 3) B 2

a Which grammar rule must be applied to 'hide' before adding the 'ing' **suffix**?

Verb ✗

b Find another word in the text that has followed this rule. flying ◯ 2

12 Explain, in your own words, why water is more likely to freeze in a pan than in half a cocoa-nut. B 3

Because the cocoa-nut works as an insulator. ◯ 2

13 What do you think is meant by these words as they are used in the text? B 2

a bore (line 57) Bore means make +

b rim (line 58) Rim is the outer skirting ① 2 of something

14 What type of reader do you think this text has been written for? Support your B 2 answer with evidence from the text.

A reader that likes to birdwatch because it reads 'you will be 2 2 able to notice the difference between the big-missel thrush & the smaller brown...'

13

15 Tick the TWO types of food that the author does not recommend as ingredients for birds' meals.

A Pieces of bread. ☐

B A range of insects. ✓

C Scraps of winter greens. ☒

D Apple peel. ☐

E Corn-on-the-cob. ✓

16 Birds only need feeding in the winter. How far do you agree with this statement? Refer to the text in your answer.

I think this statement is true because the birds seem fine with what they've got until it hits hard winter. Evidence is 'They do not so much mind the cold, but often die in hard winter.'

Now go to the Progress Chart to record your score! Total 25 35

14

Extract A

The Fox and the Crow

One day the sly, old fox went out for a walk when he saw a crow in the top of the
tree. The crow was the scruffiest old bird with tatty feathers and a scrawny head,
but she had an enormous chunk of cheese in her beak and the cheese smelled
so good to the hungry fox. The fox thought carefully about how he could get the
cheese and said to the crow: 5
   "Kind crow, clever crow, you are the most beautifully elegant bird in all of the
world. Your feathers are as glossy as ebony, your intelligence is greater than all
other creatures, but it is your voice, your unforgettable, beautiful voice that is
sweeter than the nightingale and as pretty as a picture. I do so love to hear your
voice so will you sing me your prettiest song?"   10
   The crow was delighted to hear such praise. She shook her tatty feathers, lifted
her scrawny head and opened her beak wide to begin her squawking. Down fell
the chunk of cheese into the open mouth of the crafty fox. He snapped his teeth
together. Snap! Snap! Snap! And the cheese was gone. The fox licked his lips and
looked up at the dismayed crow.   15
   "You silly crow. I am the cleverest creature in the whole world, for I knew how to
trick you. Your pride was your downfall and my prize fell down to me!"

Extract B

The Fox and the Cat

Now this same fox was boasting to a cat about how many ways he had for
escaping the enemy. He remarked, "Oh you're the stupidest cat. You can only climb
up trees, but I have a whole bag of tricks that makes me the brightest creature in
the whole world."
   At that, a pack of hunting dogs came bounding towards them with their teeth   5
gnashing hungrily and their eyes burning brightly. The clever cat scampered up the
tree and avoided the terrible onslaught. She looked down at the fox and said, "Well
this is my plan. What are you going to do?"
   The fox thought through all of his clever ways as the dogs got closer and closer
but alas, he was caught up in his own confusion and the dogs had their prey.   10

Extract C

The Fox and the Stork

The fox found that he got on well with a stork, so one day he invited the stork to
his home for a meal. The stork was very excited and turned up feeling very hungry.
The fox decided to play a cruel joke on the poor stork by serving some soup on a
shallow plate. The fox sat at the table licking up the soup saying, "Oh how delicious
this soup is, are you enjoying it, Stork?"   5

The stork had such a long beak that she couldn't eat any of the soup at all; she
could only dip the very end of her beak into it. The fox made the joke worse by
saying, "Oh Stork, I am sorry that you do not like my lovely soup. You have left all of
it! Perhaps you are not hungry?"

The stork calmly replied, "Please do not apologise, Fox, I am sure that your soup   10
is very tasty. I look forward to you coming to my house tomorrow as I am making a
fine stew."

The greedy fox looked forward to visiting the stork as he had heard about the
lovely food that she cooked. As he knocked on the stork's door he could smell the
most wonderful aroma and he licked his lips with glee. The stork let the fox in and   15
ushered him to the table. The fox could hardly wait as the clever stork brought to
the table two of the longest jars that the fox had ever seen, and they were full of the
tastiest stew. The stork could easily fit her long beak into the jar as she supped the
hot food. The fox could see and smell the food, but his snout would not fit into the
jar. All he could do was watch the stork consume the delightful fare.   20

"Ah my dear Fox," said the stork, "what goes around comes around!"

From *Aesop's fables*; adaptations by Michellejoy Hughes

These questions are about Extract A.

1 Why did the fox want the crow's cheese?

_____

2 Underline the TWO words from the list below that best describe the crow's
character.

humble   vain   modest   conceited   extravagant

3 Find an alternative word for these terms, as they are used in the text.

a dismayed (line 15) _____   b scrawny (line 12) _____

4 Each quote below is an example of a literary technique. Join each phrase to the
technique it represents.

a "as pretty as a picture ..."   **alliteration**

b "Snap! Snap! Snap! And the cheese was gone ..."   **simile**

c "Kind crow, clever crow ..."   **onomatopoeia**

16

5 Find another example of a **simile** in the text.

_____

These questions are about Extract B.

6 Underline the word in brackets that is closest in meaning to each word as it is used in the text.

    a scampered (line 6)   (darted, sidled, crept, struggled, strode)

    b alas (line 10)   (despite, sadly, because, regretful, although)

7 Find TWO **homophones** in this phrase. Write them, with their **homophone** partners, below.

    '... he was caught up in his own confusion ...'

    a _____ / _____   **b** _____ / _____

8 Explain the phrase 'a whole bag of tricks' (line 3, as used in the extract).

_____

_____

9 What do you think this tale teaches the reader?

_____

_____

_____

These questions are about Extract C.

10 Reread the phrase 'what goes around comes around' (line 21).

    a Which literary technique is this phrase an example of? _____

    b Explain what the phrase means in your own words.

_____

_____

11 Why do you think the stork is referred to as 'clever'? (line 16)

_____

_____

_____

These questions are about all three extracts.

12 These three tales are called 'fables'. Write your own definition of a fable.

_____

_____

13 Why do you think the author has used a fox in all three tales?

_____

_____

_____

_____

14 Use the information given in each tale to write a description of the fox in your own words. Refer to the text in your answer.

_____

_____

_____

_____

15 The fox thinks that the crow is vain, the cat is stupid and the stork has no feelings. Do you think his opinion of each animal is correct? Explain your answer.

_____

_____

_____

_____

_____

16 The author includes several **superlatives** in the texts. Find THREE examples, one from each extract.

a From Extract A: _____

b From Extract B: _____

c From Extract C: _____

Chapter 1 Grandfather and the Children and the Chair

Grandfather had been sitting in his old arm-chair all that pleasant afternoon, while the children were pursuing their various sports far off or near at hand. Sometimes you would have said, "Grandfather is asleep;" but still, even when his eyes were closed, his thoughts were with the young people, playing among the flowers and shrubbery of the garden.   5

He heard the voice of Laurence, who had taken possession of a heap of decayed branches which the gardener had lopped from the fruit-trees, and was building a little hut for his cousin Clara and himself. He heard Clara's gladsome voice, too, as she weeded and watered the flower-bed which had been given her for her own. He could have counted every footstep that Charley took, as he trundled his wheelbarrow   10
along the gravel-walk. And though Grandfather was old and gray-haired, yet his heart leaped with joy whenever little Alice came fluttering, like a butterfly, into the room. Sire had made each of the children her playmate in turn, and now made Grandfather her playmate too, and thought him the merriest of them all.

At last the children grew weary of their sports, because a summer afternoon is   15
like a long lifetime to the young. So they came into the room together, and clustered round Grandfather's great chair. Little Alice, who was hardly five years old, took the privilege of the youngest, and climbed his knee. It was a pleasant thing to behold that fair and golden-haired child in the lap of the old man, and to think that, different as they were, the hearts of both could be gladdened with the same joys.   20

"Grandfather," said little Alice, laying her head back upon his arm, "I am very tired now. You must tell me a story to make me go to sleep."

"That is not what story-tellers like," answered Grandfather, smiling. "They are better satisfied when they can keep their auditors awake."

"But here are Laurence, and Charley, and I," cried cousin Clara, who was twice   25
as old as little Alice. "We will all three keep wide awake. And pray, Grandfather, tell us a story about this strange-looking old chair."

Now, the chair in which Grandfather sat was made of oak, which had grown dark with age, but had been rubbed and polished till it shone as bright as mahogany. It was very large and heavy, and had a back that rose high above Grandfather's white   30
head. This back was curiously carved in open work, so as to represent flowers, and foliage, and other devices, which the children had often gazed at, but could never understand what they meant. On the very tip-top of the chair, over the head of Grandfather himself, was a likeness of a lion's head, which had such a savage grin that you would almost expect to hear it growl and snarl.   35

The children had seen Grandfather sitting in this chair ever since they could remember anything. Perhaps the younger of them supposed that he and the chair had come into the world together, and that both had always been as old as they were now. At this time, however, it happened to be the fashion for ladies to adorn their drawing-rooms with the oldest and oddest chairs that could be found.   40
It seemed to cousin Clara that, if these ladies could have seen Grandfather's old chair, they would have thought it worth all the rest together. She wondered if it were

not even older than Grandfather himself, and longed to know all about its history.

"Do, Grandfather, talk to us about this chair," she repeated.

"Well, child," said Grandfather, patting Clara's cheek, "I can tell you a great many 45
stories of my chair. Perhaps your cousin Laurence would like to hear them too.
They would teach him something about the history and distinguished people of his
country which he has never read in any of his schoolbooks."

Cousin Laurence was a boy of twelve, a bright scholar, in whom an early
thoughtfulness and sensibility began to show themselves. His young fancy kindled 50
at the idea of knowing all the adventures of this venerable chair. He looked eagerly
in Grandfather's face; and even Charley, a bold, brisk, restless little fellow of nine,
sat himself down on the carpet, and resolved to be quiet for at least ten minutes,
should the story last so long.

Meantime, little Alice was already asleep; so Grandfather, being much pleased with 55
such an attentive audience, began to talk about matters that happened long ago.

From *Grandfather's Chair* by Nathaniel Hawthorne

1 List the children's names in age order, from oldest to youngest.

B | 2

_____

1

2 Was Clara happy as she tended to the flower-bed? Explain your answer with
reference to the text.

B | 2

_____

_____

2

3 Tick the TWO statements that are true.

B | 2

A The chair was worth a lot of money. ☐

B Grandfather had brown hair. ☐

C Clara and Laurence were cousins. ☐

D Alice slept during Grandfather's story. ☐

E Grandfather rarely sat in the chair. ☐

2

4 Explain, in your own words, why the children 'grew weary of their sports'
(line 15).

B | 3

_____

_____

_____

2

5 Which phrase suggests that Grandfather was pleased to have Alice sitting on his knee?

_____

6 Describe Grandfather's chair in your own words.

_____

_____

_____

_____

7 Give an alternative for each word as it is used in the text.

a lopped (line 7) _____   **b** savage (line 34) _____

8 Find an example of each of the following parts of speech in this sentence.

'It was very large and heavy, and had a back that rose high above Grandfather's white head.'

a a **noun** _____   **b** an **adjective** _____

c a **pronoun** _____   **d** a **preposition** _____

9 Find TWO examples of **similes** in the text.

_____

_____

10 Grandfather had bought the chair recently. Do you agree with this statement? Support your answer with evidence from the text.

_____

_____

_____

11 Find THREE **homophones** in this sentence. Write them, with their **homophone** partners, below.

"I can tell you a great many stories of my chair."

a _____ / _____   **b** _____ / _____

c _____ / _____

12 Why do you think the children wanted Grandfather to tell them a story?

_____

_____

_____

_____

3

13 What do you think Grandfather means when he says that the stories would teach Laurence "something about the history and distinguished people of his country which he has never read in any of his schoolbooks" (lines 47–48)?

_____

_____

_____

_____

3

14 What type of story do you think Grandfather will tell? Use the text to support your answer.

_____

_____

_____

_____

3

Now go to the Progress Chart to record your score! **Total** 35

The Gods of Greece

The Greeks believed that the world was round and flat. Its outer border was the great river, Ocean. The Mediterranean Sea was in the centre of this circle.

Far to the North lived the Hyperboreans in a beautiful land where cold winds did not blow and snow never fell. These people were not obliged to work, and they had no enemies with whom to fight. Sickness and old age did not trouble them. Their lives were happy and tranquil. 5

In the distant South were the Æthiopians, who were so good and happy that the gods often went to visit them.

In the far-off West were the Fortunate Isles, or 'Islands of the Blessed', where everything was charming, and where a few people, beloved by the gods, lived forever without pain or sorrow. 10

The Greeks thought there were many gods, most of whom lived above the clouds on top of Olympus, a mountain in Thessaly. They had bodies like men and women, but they were larger, stronger, and usually handsomer than human beings.

The king of all the gods, and the father of many of them, was called Zeus. The Latin name for this god is Jupiter. He was the ruler of the weather. At his command the clouds gathered, rain or snow fell, gentle winds blew, or storms roared. He darted lightning across the sky and hurled thunderbolts upon the world. 15

The tallest trees and highest mountain peaks were sacred to him.

He was also the god of justice, and sent his servants, the Furies, to punish men and women who did wrong. 20

His wife was Hera, who in Latin is called Juno. She was very handsome and stately. Her eyes were large and dark, so that one poet called her 'ox-eyed'. She was proud and quarrelsome and ready to harm those who made her angry.

This couple had several children. One of them, Hephæstus, the Latin Vulcanus, is said by some to have been born lame. Others say that his father in a fit of anger threw him out of heaven. He fell for a long summer day, and when he reached the island of Lemnos he had little life remaining in him, and limped forever after. He was the blacksmith god, who built houses for the other gods and made the sceptre of Zeus, the arrows used by Apollo and Artemis, and other wonderful things. He was good-natured and fond of fun, but not foolish. Volcanoes were called his earthly workshops. 25 30

His wife was Aphrodite, the Latin Venus, the loveliest of all the goddesses, who was said to have been born from the foam of the sea. She was the ruler of love and beauty. Wherever she went soft and gentle breezes followed her, and flowers sprang up where her feet touched. She made some people happy, but for others she caused much grief and trouble. 35

One day Zeus had a terrible headache. Hephæstus, with an axe, split open his father's aching head. The goddess Athene, the Latin Minerva, sprang out, full grown and dressed in armour. She became the goddess of wisdom, and also took care of cities. She never married but lived alone in her house upon Mount Olympus. 40

Phœbus, the Latin Apollo, was the god who ruled the sun. He loved music and poetry.

Artemis, the Latin Diana, was his twin sister. She had charge of the moon and was the friend of the hunters.

Hermes, the Latin Mercurius, whence our Mercury, was handsome and swift, the messenger of the gods. Under his care were merchants, travellers, and public speakers. He wore a low-crowned hat with wings, and wings grew from his ankles. In his hand, he carried a wand around which snakes twined. He was very cunning and full of tricks.

Ares, the Latin Mars, was the god of war, finding pleasure in battle and death.

Hestia, the Latin Vesta, was the sister of Zeus. She was the goddess of the fireside and watched over the homes of men. She never married, but Zeus gave her a seat in the centre of his palace and sent her the sweetest morsels at every feast. On earth she was worshipped as the oldest and best of the gods. In her temple a sacred fire was kept forever burning, watched by un-married women, who were called 'Vestal Virgins'.

These ten gods formed the 'Great Council' of Olympus. They lived in their own houses of brass, built by Hephæstus, but every day they went to the palace of Zeus and feasted on ambrosia and nectar. Hebe, the beautiful daughter of Zeus and Hera, waited upon the table. After her marriage to Heracles her place was taken by Ganymede, a beautiful Trojan boy, whom Zeus in the form of an eagle carried away to heaven. At the feasts Apollo played on his lyre and the Muses sang. The Muses were nine sisters, who lived on Mount Parnassus. They had charge of poetry, history, music, tragedy, comedy, dancing, love-songs, hymns, and astronomy.

The ruler of the sea was Poseidon, whose Latin name was Neptune. Under the waves he had a shining palace, the work of Hephæstus.

Demeter, the Latin Ceres, was goddess of the earth, especially of harvests of grain. Dionysus, or Bacchus, was the god of vineyards and wine, and was particularly adored by the Greeks. Eros, the Latin Cupid, the little god of love, was the son of Venus. Eos was the goddess of the dawn. Iris was the messenger of Hera, and the road by which she travelled from heaven to earth was the rainbow, which vanished when her errand was done.

There were three Fates, who spun the thread of human life and cut it off at their pleasure.

There were three Graces, who favoured everything beautiful and charming in manners and dress.

There were also three Furies, who had snakes for hair and were frightful to look at. It was their duty to follow wicked men and women and punish them with dreadful whips.

Nemesis, like the Furies, pursued those who had done wrong, particularly those who had insulted the gods. Wherever she went trouble and sorrow followed. Momus was the god of laughter, Morpheus of sleep, and Plutus of riches. Plutus was blind and could not see those to whom he gave his gifts. When he approached men he limped slowly along. When he left them he flew away.

All these went and came as they pleased, being sometimes in the sky, sometimes on the earth. They did not always do right, and they often quarrelled and fought among themselves. Although they could not be killed, they could be wounded. Then ichor instead of blood flowed from their veins. They took much interest in human affairs; they had their favourites whom they helped, and their enemies whom they tried to harm.

From *Stories of the Ancient Greeks* by Charles D. Shaw

1 Choose ONE word or short phrase from the list below that best completes each of the following sentences.

North   Mediterranean   East   West   Hyperboreans   Æthiopians

Fortunate Isles   Thessaly   South   Ganymede   Mount Parnassus

a The lands to the extreme left were called the _____ .

b The people who lived at the most northern point were the _____ .

c The Greeks believed that the very middle of the world was the _____ .

d The Æthiopians lived to the far _____ .

2 Did the gods ever come down from the skies? Support your answer with TWO pieces of evidence from the text.

_____

_____

3 What is the Greek name for the god Jupiter? _____

4 In which part of the world did some people enjoy eternal life?

_____

5 Write your own description of Hera's physical appearance and her personality.

_____

_____

_____

_____

_____

6 Explain the sentence, 'Volcanoes were called his earthly workshops …', as used in the text (line 31).

_____

_____

7 Aphrodite was always kind and compassionate. Do you agree with this statement? Refer to the text in your answer.

_____

_____

_____

8 Tick the TWO statements that are false.

B 2

A Artemis was the twin sister of Diana. ☐

B Hermes was crafty. ☐

C Nemesis made people laugh. ☐

D Zeus was the brother of Hestia. ☐

E Hephæstus was Cupid's father. ☐

2

9 If you held one of the following professions during this time, which god would have been most important to you?

B 2

a a trader _____ b a farmer _____

2

10 Give an alternative for each word as it is used in the text.

B 2

a hurled (line 18) _____ b morsels (line 53) _____

2

11 What material was Apollo's house made from?

B 2

_____

1

12 Reread lines 20–21 and 77–79 about the Furies.

B 2

a Describe the role of the Furies in your own words.

_____

_____

2

b Why do you think that the Furies looked so frightening?

_____

_____

1

13 This mythological extract illustrates several ways in which the Greek gods were different from humans. Explain at least EIGHT of these differences, referring to the text to support your answer.

B 2

_____

_____

_____

_____

_____

_____

_____

8

Now go to the Progress Chart to record your score!   Total 35

Paper 7

Chapter 1 The Black-Bellied Tarantula

Lycosa tarantula by preference inhabits open places, dry, arid, uncultivated places, exposed to the sun. She lives generally – at least when full-grown – in underground passages, regular burrows, which she digs for herself. These burrows are cylindrical; they are often an inch in diameter and run into the ground to a depth of more than a foot; but they are not perpendicular. The inhabitant of this gut proves that she is at the same time a skilful hunter and an able engineer. It was a question for her not only of constructing a deep retreat that could hide her from the pursuit of her foes: she also had to set up her observatory whence to watch for her prey and dart out upon it. The Tarantula provides for every contingency: the underground passage, in fact, begins by being vertical, but, at four or five inches from the surface, it bends at an obtuse angle, forms a horizontal turning and then becomes perpendicular once more. It is at the elbow of this tunnel that the Tarantula posts herself as a vigilant sentry and does not for a moment lose sight of the door of her dwelling; it was there that, at the period when I was hunting her, I used to see those eyes gleaming like diamonds, bright as a cat's eyes in the dark.

The outer orifice of the Tarantula's burrow is usually surmounted by a shaft constructed throughout by herself. It is a genuine work of architecture, standing as much as an inch above the ground and sometimes two inches in diameter, so that it is wider than the burrow itself. This last circumstance, which seems to have been calculated by the industrious Spider, lends itself admirably to the necessary extension of the legs at the moment when the prey is to be seized. The shaft is composed mainly of bits of dry wood joined by a little clay and so artistically laid, one above the other, that they form the scaffolding of a straight column, the inside of which is a hollow cylinder. The solidity of this tubular building, of this outwork, is ensured above all by the fact that it is lined, upholstered within, with a texture woven by the Lycosa's spinnerets and continued throughout the interior of the burrow. It is easy to imagine how useful this cleverly-manufactured lining must be for preventing landslip or warping, for maintaining cleanliness and for helping her claws to scale the fortress.

I hinted that this outwork of the burrow was not there invariably; as a matter of fact, I have often come across Tarantulas' holes without a trace of it, perhaps because it had been accidentally destroyed by the weather, or because the Lycosa may not always light upon the proper building-materials, or, lastly, because architectural talent is possibly declared only in individuals that have reached the final stage, the period of perfection of their physical and intellectual development.

One thing is certain, that I have had numerous opportunities of seeing these shafts, these outworks of the Tarantula's abode; they remind me, on a larger scale, of the tubes of certain Caddis-worms. The Arachnid had more than one object in view in constructing them: she shelters her retreat from the floods; she protects it from the fall of foreign bodies which, swept by the wind, might end by obstructing it; lastly, she uses it as a snare by offering the Flies and other insects whereon she feeds a projecting point to settle on. Who shall tell us all the wiles employed by this clever and daring huntress?

45

From *The Life of the Spider* by Jean Henri Fabre

1 What type of home does the adult Lycosa tarantula live in?

_____

2 Which TWO skills does the Tarantula possess?

_____

_____

3 Where specifically does the spider lie in wait for her victims?

_____

4 What information are you given about the Tarantula's diet?

_____

5 Underline the word in brackets that is closest in meaning to each word as it is used in the text.

   a arid (line 2)   (unpleasant, putrid, luscious, barren, dangerous)

   b perpendicular (line 9)   (vertical, horizontal, parallel, reflective, obtuse)

   c vigilant (line 17)   (fragile, ravenous, distracted, watchful, bold)

   d orifice (line 21)   (section, opening, vessel, corner, block)

6 Find TWO **similes** that the author uses in the text.

_____

_____

7 Other than the words 'Lycosa tarantula' and 'spider', which other scientific term does the author use to describe the creature?

_____

8 What helps to prevent dirt from building up in the Tarantula's home?

_____

9 You are more likely to find a Lycosa tarantula in a rainforest than in a desert. Do you agree with this statement? Explain your answer with reference to the text.

B 2

_____

_____

_____

2

10 Explain, in your own words, the THREE reasons why not all tarantulas' homes will have an outer burrow.

B 2

_____

_____

_____

_____

3

11 Which word, as used in the text, means the same as 'consistently'?

B 2

_____

1

12 Explain why tarantulas build shafts. Support your answer with THREE pieces of evidence from the text.

B 2

_____

_____

_____

_____

3

13 Why do you think the shaft is hollow rather than solid?

B 2

_____

_____

1

14 Underline a **connective** in the following sentence.

B 2

'This last circumstance, which seems to have been calculated by the industrious spider, lends itself admirably to the necessary extension of the legs at the moment when the prey is to be seized.'

1

15 What is meant by the phrase, 'The Tarantula provides for every contingency …' (line 14)?

B 2

_____

_____

_____

_____

◯ 3

16 Lycosa tarantulas are extremely clever creatures. Discuss this statement with reference to the text.

B 2

_____

_____

_____

_____

_____

_____

_____

◯ 5

17 The author refers to the spider as being 'industrious'. What do you think this means?

B 2

_____

◯ 1

18 What type of source do you think this extract has been taken from? Explain your answer.

B 1

_____

_____

_____

◯ 2

Paper 8

The Ancient Scythians

Far over the eastern half of Europe extends a vast and mighty plain, spreading thousands of miles to the north and south, to the east and west, in the north a land of forests, in the south and east a region of treeless levels. Here stretches the Black Land, whose deep dark soil is fit for endless harvests; here are the arable steppes, a vast fertile prairie land, and here again the barren steppes, fit only for 5 wandering herds and the tents of nomad shepherds. Across this great plain, in all directions, flow myriads of meandering streams, many of them swelling into noble rivers, whose waters find their outlet in great seas. Over it blow the biting winds of the Arctic zone, chaining its waters in fetters of ice for half the year. On it in summer shine warm suns, in whose enlivening rays life flows full again. 10

Such is the land with which we have to deal, Russia, the seeding-place of nations, the home of restless tribes. Here the vast level of Northern Asia spreads like a sea over half of Europe, following the lowlands between the Urals and the Caspian Sea. Over these broad plains the fierce horsemen of the East long found an easy pathway to the rich and doomed cities of the West. Russia was playing its 15 part in the grand drama of the nations in far-off days when such a land was hardly known to exist.

Have any of my readers ever from a hill-top looked out over a broad, low-lying meadow-land filled with morning mist, a dense white shroud under which everything lay hidden, all life and movement lost to view? In such a scene, as the mist thins 20 under the rays of the rising sun, vague forms at first dimly appear, magnified and monstrous in their outlines, the shadows of a buried wonderland. Then, as the mist slowly lifts, like a great white curtain, living and moving objects appear below, still of strange outlines and unnatural dimensions. Finally, as if by the sweep of an enchanter's wand, the mists vanish, the land lies clear under the solar rays, and we 25 perceive that these seeming monsters and giants are but the familiar forms which we know so well, those of houses and trees, men and their herds, actively stirring beneath us, clearly revealed as the things of every day.

It is thus that the land of Russia appears to us when the mists of prehistoric time first begin to lift. Half-formed figures appear, rising, vanishing, showing 30 large through the vapour; stirring, interwoven, endlessly coming and going; a phantasmagoria which it is impossible more than half to understand. At that early date the great Russian plain seems to have been the home of unnumbered tribes of varied race and origin, made up of men doubtless full of hopes and aspirations like ourselves, yet whose story we fail to read on the blurred page of history, and 35 concerning whom we must rest content with knowing a few of the names.

Yet progressive civilizations had long existed in the countries to the south, Egypt and Assyria, Greece and Persia. History was actively being made there, but it had not penetrated the mist-laden North. The Greeks founded colonies on the northern shores of the Black Sea, but they troubled themselves little about the seething 40 tribes with whom they came there into contact. The land they called Scythia, and its people Scythians, but the latter were scarcely known until about 500 B.C., when

Darius, the great Persian king, crossed the Danube and invaded their country. He found life there in abundance, and more war-like activity than he relished, for the fierce nomads drove him and his army in terror from their soil, and only fortune and   45
a bridge of boats saved them from perishing.

It was this event that first gave the people of old Russia a place on the page of history.

From *Historical Tales: Russian* by Charles Morris

1 Russia was north of which FOUR countries?

a _____   b _____

c _____   d _____

2 If you were a crop farmer at this time, which section of the Black Land would you have chosen for your farmland? Explain your answer with reference to the text.

_____

_____

_____

3 Which ONE word does the author use to describe the Arctic winds?

_____

4 For approximately how many months do these winds last?

_____

5 Explain the following section of text in your own words.

'… chaining its waters in fetters of ice for half the year. On it in summer shine warm suns, in whose enlivening rays life flows full again.'

_____

_____

_____

_____

6 Which TWO phrases tell the reader that Russia is the source of many nationalities?

_____

_____

7 Where are the lowlands?

_____

B 2

1

8 Reread the second paragraph.

B 2

  a Which literary technique is included in this section?

_____

  b Write out the relevant phrase.

2

_____

9 Give an alternative word for each of these words as they are used in the extract.

B 2

  a meandering (line 7) _____   **b** aspirations (line 34) _____

  c seething (line 40) _____   **d** fortune (line 45) _____

4

10 Explain, in your own words, why everyday things appear monstrous and distorted (lines 18–28). Refer to the text in your answer.

B 2

_____

_____

2

11 How does the author make the text in the third paragraph sound supernatural? Include at least FIVE pieces of evidence from the text to support your answer.

B 2

_____

_____

_____

_____

_____

5

_____

12 Choose ONE word from the group below that best completes each of the following sentences.

> North   East   South   West   Danube   Greek   Scythians
>
>   Darius   Black Sea   Persia   Caspian Sea   Russia

a The horsemen from the _____ were fierce.

b The area to the _____ was misty and impenetrable.

c The Greeks cared little for the people they named _____.

d There were rich cities in the _____ of Russia.

4

13 What event saw the Scythians enter the history books?

_____

1

14 In what type of source would you expect to find this extract? Explain your answer with reference to the text.

_____

_____

_____

2

Firefighters Fight Forest Fire

Tuesday 3rd September 2009

by Louisa Johnson

This morning, firefighters from the Cheshire fire service were still trying to control the fire that began sweeping through the ancient forestland on Sunday.

Fire chief David Barnsley remarked that 5 his crew had worked tirelessly over the last three days to put out the flames. He added, "The aim of my team has been twofold: to prevent any further damage to the forest and to stop the fire from spreading to nearby 10 homes. It's still too early to say whether people or animals have been caught up in the blaze. We don't yet know the initial cause of the inferno, but the unusually dry weather and recent heatwave could have caused the 15 fallen leaves to ignite. At this stage, we are also not ruling out the possibility of, for example, arson or a careless camper. The fire sprang up like a coiled spring, engulfing several acres within minutes. As a result, we 20 are doubtful that any casualties caught up in the blaze will have survived, but we are continuing our search."

When asked for his view on this devastating event, local resident Mr Morgan, a member 25 of the Woodland Trust, commented, "I walk my dog in my local forest every day and I regularly see smokers flicking cigarette ash without, it seems, a second thought. I have also seen campers lighting open fires in small 30 clearings, groups of people having barbecues in the summer and teenagers setting off their own fireworks and lighting bonfires on Bonfire Night. All of these people have chosen to ignore the warning notices that the 35 Woodland Trust have posted around the area. It is clear that these offenders don't take the time to consider the fact that every match, cigarette end, fire or barbecue ember or firework has the potential to destroy a whole 40 woodland."

Mr Morgan continued, "Some of the trees in this area were over a hundred years old and they have been destroyed within minutes. The forest was also brimming with wildlife: 45 rabbits, birds, foxes, badgers, hedgehogs and squirrels, which have now either been lost to the flames or have been made homeless through the destruction of their habitat."

Cheshire police have issued another urgent 50 public warning, reminding everyone of the dangers of heatwaves as well as general fire safety tips and have also asked all visitors to the county's many forests and woodlands to be extra vigilant. If members of the public 55 come across any further outbreaks of forest fires or see anyone acting suspiciously, they should report the incident at their local police station, fire service, or Woodland Trust office immediately. 60

B

Fireworks Sold to 10-year-old

Jason Jenkins, vendor of 'Newz' in Primrose Crescent, was fined £300 and ordered to pay £200 costs within 28 days when he appeared before Cheshire magistrates. He was prosecuted after a joint council and Cheshire fire and rescue service operation was conducted in the run-up to last year's Bonfire Night. On 27th October, a 10-year-old child volunteer was able to purchase fireworks from the store. Under-18s are banned from buying fireworks. 10

Councillor Derek Jones commented, "This case is a good example of how seriously we take this issue and acts as a warning for other tempted vendors. We will always prosecute anyone who sells fireworks illegally." 15

Shirley Bryan, spokeswoman for Sparkless, the anti-firework lobby, observed, "This is another great day for the many people who want to see a complete ban on fireworks being available to the public." She added, "Children 20 are hurt every year and many fires are directly caused through the sale of fireworks. We want them to be made illegal for all citizens, not just the under-18s."

C

19th November 2008   PC Amarjit Khan 20785

At 20:14 I was called to 119 Harrogate Avenue by Mrs Leona Brahms who reported smelling toxic fumes coming from the direction of the neighbouring property.

On approach, 117 Harrogate Avenue appeared derelict and in a poor state of repair.

Upon closer investigation I found 13-year-old Callum Crockett attempting to pull his sister, 11-year-old Madison, through a downstairs front window amid plumes of black 5 smoke and noxious fumes. Madison appeared confused so I radioed for an ambulance and then ensured that she was comfortable on the front lawn. At this point, Callum calmly confirmed that no other person was in the derelict property; further stating that 10-year-old Meera Davis had been in the property with them but had made an earlier escape to raise the alarm at home. The arrival of Meera and her mother, Mrs Janine Davis of 72 10 Leeds Road, coincided with that of the ambulance. Mrs Davis provided additional address and contact details for her sister, Ms Jodie Crockett; mother to both Callum and Madison.

All three children, accompanied by myself and Mrs Davis, were transferred to Alder Hey Children's Hospital at 20:35. Ms Crockett arrived at the hospital at 21:10. At 21:40 I was able to question both Callum and Meera further about the incident. They informed 15 me that they often play at the derelict house. On this occasion, Callum found a box of matches in a kitchen cupboard and decided to light a fire to keep them all warm in the downstairs front room. He made a heap from the post that littered the hallway and proceeded to light it. The paper caught quickly and the fire soon spread to the remains of the armchair. The flames died out soon after reaching the chair (Callum recalls the chair 20 being wet) but the chair then appeared to emit thick, black smoke which blocked the path to the front exit.

Callum then smashed the front window with a broken table leg, and instructed Meera to crawl out and go for help. It was at this point that Callum noticed Madison becoming drowsy. He acted quickly in order to pull her through the broken window into the air. 25

Meera and Callum were released from Alder Hey at 21:50. Madison is being kept in for observation. Her condition was described by doctors as stable and not critical.

PC Amarjit Khan   19/11/2008 23:42

These questions are about Extract A.

1 What date did the forest fire start?

_____

2 Describe, in your own words, the THREE possible ways in which David Barnsley
  thinks the fire could have been triggered.

_____

_____

_____

3 Which literary technique is the title of Extract A an example of?

_____

4 Find two **synonyms** for the word 'fire' in the second paragraph.

_____

5 Why do you think Mr Morgan feels that setting off fireworks in woodland is
  dangerous?

_____

_____

_____

_____

6 Each extract has been taken from a different source. Where do you think Extract
  A has been taken from? Support your answer with FIVE pieces of evidence.

_____

_____

_____

_____

_____

These questions are about Extract B.

7 What had Jason Jenkins done wrong?

_____

_____

8 What does the phrase 'other tempted vendors' (lines 13–14) mean?

_____

_____

9 Tick the ONE statement that is true.

A Councillor Derek Jones lives in Primrose Crescent. ☐

B John Jenkins had to pay £500. ☐

C Under-18s are banned from entering shops that sell fireworks. ☐

D The council is working with the fire service. ☐

E Everyone who sells fireworks will be prosecuted. ☐

F A 10-year-old was paid to buy fireworks from 'Newz'. ☐

10 Describe, in your own words, what Sparkless believes in.

_____

_____

11 Give an alternative word or short phrase for each of these words as used in the text.

a conducted (line 6) _____   **b** citizens (line 23) _____

These questions are about Extract C.

12 How do you know that the smoke was dangerous? Refer to the text in your answer.

_____

_____

_____

13 What stopped the fire from spreading?

_____

14 Why do you think it was easy for Callum to start a fire? Explain your answer with reference to the text.

B 2

_____

_____

_____

2

15 Callum obviously had an irresponsible nature. Do you agree with this statement? Support your answer with evidence from the text.

B 2

_____

_____

_____

_____

4

This question is based on all three extracts.

16 'Children should be taught about the dangers of fire from an early age.' If you were teaching fire safety to a Year 5 class, what would be the FIVE key points you would want to teach them and why? You can use any or all of these extracts to help you explain your answer.

B 3

_____

_____

_____

_____

_____

_____

_____

_____

_____

5

Now go to the Progress Chart to record your score! **Total** **35**

The Questing Beast

BUT Arthur had many battles to fight and many Kings to conquer before he was acknowledged lord of them all, and often he would have failed had he not listened to the wisdom of Merlin, and been helped by his sword Excalibur, which in obedience to Merlin's orders he never drew till things were going ill with him. Later it shall be told how the King got the sword Excalibur, which shone so bright in his enemies' eyes that they fell back, dazzled by the brightness. Many Knights came to his standard, and among them Sir Ban, King of Gaul beyond the sea, who was ever his faithful friend. And it was in one of these wars, when King Arthur and King Ban and King Bors went to the rescue of the King of Cameliard, that Arthur saw Guenevere, the King's daughter, whom he afterwards wedded. By and by King Ban and King Bors returned to their own country across the sea, and the King went to Carlion, a town on the river Usk, where a strange dream came to him.

He thought that the land was over-run with gryphons and serpents which burnt and slew his people, and he made war on the monsters, and was sorely wounded, though at last he killed them all. When he awoke the remembrance of his dream was heavy upon him, and to shake it off he summoned his Knights to hunt with him, and they rode fast till they reached a forest. Soon they spied a hart before them, which the King claimed as his game, and he spurred his horse and rode after him. But the hart ran fast and the King could not get near it, and the chase lasted so long that the King himself grew heavy and his horse fell dead under him. Then he sat under a tree and rested, till he heard the baying of hounds, and fancied he counted as many as thirty of them. He raised his head to look, and, coming towards him, saw a beast so strange that its like was not to be found throughout his kingdom. It went straight to the well and drank, making as it did so the noise of many hounds baying, and when it had drunk its fill the beast went its way.

While the King was wondering what sort of a beast this could be, a Knight rode by, who, seeing a man lying under a tree, stopped and said to him: "Knight full of thought and sleepy, tell me if a strange beast has passed this way?"

"Yes, truly," answered Arthur, "and by now it must be two miles distant. What do you want with it?"

"Oh sir, I have followed that beast from far," replied he, "and have ridden my horse to death. If only I could find another I would still go after it." As he spoke a squire came up leading a fresh horse for the King, and when the Knight saw it he prayed that it might be given to him, "for," said he, "I have followed this quest this twelvemonth, and either I shall slay him or he will slay me."

"Sir Knight," answered the King, "you have done your part; leave now your quest, and let me follow the beast for the same time that you have done." 45

"Ah, fool!" replied the Knight, whose name was Pellinore, "it would be all in vain, for none may slay that beast but I or my next of kin," and without more words he sprang into the saddle. "You may take my horse by force," said the King, "but I should like to prove first which of us two is the better horseman."

"Well," answered the Knight, "when you want me, come to this spring. Here you 50 will always find me," and, spurring his horse, he galloped away. The King watched him till he was out of sight, then turned to his squire and bade him bring another horse as quickly as he could. While he was waiting for it the wizard Merlin came along in the likeness of a boy, and asked the King why he was so thoughtful.

"I may well be thoughtful," replied the King, "for I have seen the most wonderful 55 sight in all the world."

"That I know well," said Merlin, "for I know all your thoughts. But it is folly to let your mind dwell on it, for thinking will mend nothing. I know, too, that, Uther Pendragon was your father, and your mother was the Lady Igraine."

"How can a boy like you know that?" cried Arthur, growing angry; but Merlin only 60 answered, "I know it better than any man living," and passed, returning soon after in the likeness of an old man of fourscore, and sitting down by the well to rest. "What makes you so sad?" asked he.

"I may well be sad," replied Arthur, "there is plenty to make me so. And besides, there was a boy here who told me things that he had no business to know, and 65 among them the names of my father and mother."

"He told you the truth," said the old man, "and if you would have listened he could have told you still more: how that your sister shall have a child who shall destroy you and all your Knights."

"Who are you?" asked Arthur, wondering. 70

"I am Merlin, and it was I who came to you in the likeness of a boy. I know all things; how that you shall die a noble death, being slain in battle, while my end will be shameful, for I shall be put alive into the earth."

There was no time to say more, for the man brought up the King's horse and he mounted, and rode fast till he came to Carlion. 75

From *King Arthur: Tales of the Round Table* edited by Andrew Lang

1 How many kings are mentioned in the extract?

B 2

1

_____

2 Tick the TWO statements that are true.

B 2

A The King's enemies were stabbed by his sword. ☐

B Guenevere married King Bors. ☐

C Sir Ban was dazzled by Excalibur's brightness. ☐

D King Bors lived abroad. ☐

E The King of Gaul helped the King of Cameliard. ☐

2

3 Choose ONE word or short phrase from the group below that best completes each of the following sentences.

the hart   Arthur   Guenevere   King Bors   Excalibur   Merlin

Sir Ban   Carlion   Usk   gryphons   hounds   The Knight

a The King of Gaul was called _____ .

b The town on the river Usk was called _____ .

c In the dream, the land was over-run with _____ .

4 Give TWO reasons why Arthur was successful in battle.

_____

_____

_____

5 Explain why the King chose to go hunting. Support your answer with evidence from the text.

_____

_____

_____

6 What is meant by '… the King claimed as his game …' (line 26)?

_____

_____

_____

7 Find an example of each of the following parts of speech in this sentence.

'Then he sat under a tree and rested, till he heard the baying of hounds, and fancied he counted as many as thirty of them.'

a a **pronoun** _____   **b** a **preposition** _____

c a **conjunction** _____

8 Why did Pellinore call the King a fool?

_____

_____

_____

9 Give an alternative for each word as it is used in the text.

a acknowledged (line 3) _____ **b** baying (line 29) _____

c quest (line 42) _____ **d** likeness (line 54) _____

10 In the extract, the word 'fancied' is written in the **past tense** (line 29).

a Which grammar rule must be applied to the **present tense** form of this word to change it into the **past tense** as shown?

_____

_____

b Find another word in the text that has followed this rule. Write the word in its **present tense** form.

_____

11 For how long did the King intend to pursue the beast?

_____

12 Who were Arthur's parents?

_____

13 Explain, in your own words, the difference between how Merlin foresaw Arthur's death and his own.

_____

_____

_____

_____

14 This extract is not taken from a modern text. Find ONE word or short phrase in each of the sections listed below that supports this statement.

a (line 43) _____ **b** (line 52) _____

c (line 62) _____

15 This extract is from an adventure story. Do you agree with this statement? Support your answer with THREE pieces of evidence from the text.

_____

_____

_____

_____

Progress Chart Fourth papers in Comprehension

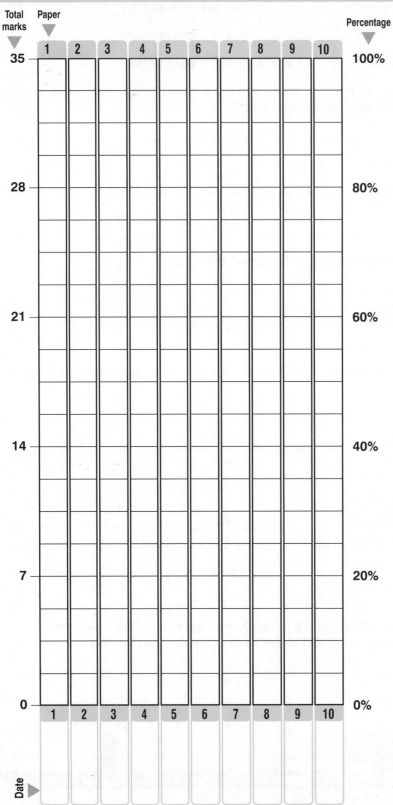

When you've finished the book use the Next Steps Planner